THE SVETA'S ART PHENOMENON

Sveta's art is a state of consciousness as much as it is paper, pencils, and paint. How one can define this phenomenon?
I considered myself fit to write about her art as I studied art
all my life. First, as an artist, through countless art studios and five years of an art college, then as an art historian, as a philosopher of art, and then as a Jungian psychologist and philosopher.
And now, looking at her addictive, colorful pages, I am at total loss.
I am in awe. It is deeper than day can comprehend, to borrow Nietzsche's expression, and layered with meaning one usually does not expect to find in art.
First of all, Sveta's art is aesthetically beautiful. The composition, the flow and interaction of forms, the visual balance of the color are true. Her sense of when enough is enough is superb. She walks the line between painting too sketchy and over-perfecting the detail with taste and grace. Her mastery of form, the ability to make it speak just what was intended is dynamic and refined.
Is Sveta also a colorist? Definitely; the colors come on the paper, like the forms do: freely, unpredictably, in their endless expressive variety. But, Sveta possesses tasteful and well-measured-out rigor, using the colors just so.
There is also a certain aesthetically pleasing economy in her work with shapes and colors. Paul Klee said that making art is simple: it's just putting the right color in the right place. This is exactly what Sveta does.

Her myth got God. It is not the God of a specific religion, of theological arguments, and not an abstract, fully transcendent Creator. It is not all-good, honey-sweet God, not the God of a specific gender, or with a specific name or agenda; not a judgmental, endlessly superior, all-knowing one. It is very homey, even shy, and kind God, who does not know Him/Herself very well, but does understand flawed human condition. And at the same time, this God is "fully other," as Mircea Eliade has it, and fully numinous—the real thing. It is the God who can only be super-personal, and come to each person in a unique way. It is a very simple and unpretentious God, who is just this: living meaning.

This God is both, the ultimate subject and creator of Sveta's art. If you do not grasp such God, fine: go and find your own meaning. This is, I think, the main message of her art; at least, it is what I receive from it the most vividly: it gives me a sturdy sense of the presence of meaning.
Like her God, Sveta's art is homey, warm, approachable, and kind. We all may be fans of Alex Gray and even H.R Gigerâ speaking of the spiritual, the imaginative, the channeling type of art. But, we definitely can use some kindness on canvas. Sveta's art has a confident and distinct voice, and it speaks kindness.

The big orange Self, sitting with Its hands over Its knees, with small Sveta on Its shoulder, together looking at the mountains (because they are not yet on speaking terms, says Sveta); two rectangular-ish shapes, one red and another white, smiling and holding hands; a dainty woman with a huge lit cigarette in a black dress and white beret, her white wings hang helplessly down. The images are quintessential art: they are images in their own right, with life and meaning of their own.

Non of these may make immediate sense to us: Sveta paints not to please the viewer, but to express her inferiority, intense with meaning that is beyond common sense. Her images seem to be a wonder for her as much as they are for us.

She is far from capitalizing on a once-found form, combination of colors, or plot: the art pieces range widely in style from simple and economic to elegant and sophisticated depending on the needs of the life-forms of the archetypal realm asking for expression.

Freud famously said that dreams are the royal road to the Unconscious. Jung added that active imagination is also a very good way to the realm of the ultimate mystery. Sveta's art works are a happy marriage of both: the ideas, images, and colors spill freely from the radically Unknown, being Its messengers and speaking Its language. Sveta belongs with imaginative and channeling branch of artists, but not with Dali, Magritte, and Giger. Her flock is Marc Chagall, Mikalojus Eiurlionis, Niko Pirosmani. As an artist, she is direct, spontaneous, fresh, genuine, and confidently dances the line between purity and naivete. Her art is both extremely personal and completely transpersonal. That is why, I think, it flows so freely.
OLENA PROVENCHER

"Scream for Borisov" - Luda my sister, was in a hospital with cyst inside her head, which was about to burst out.

Borisov her husband, was next to her. When he went out she called me and said:

Imagine he shows me videos having sex with his lover Yana. She was too week and too scared. You don't know him Sveta. He NEVER forgets anything. Not a little thing. He comes with sophisticated psychological tortures and it's his food and air and joy and blood.

I went to the sky. When he came into her room I screamed: Luda next to you is a man who wants your cyst to burst out.

He ran away.

10 years of Nazi tortures. Confused and scared to death our little naive girl in the jell captured by monster.

This is in her memory and to all who goes through abuse in fear.

When she was standing in front him, barefoot, with cut head, just after yet another operation, he happily exclaimed: I am loved! Somebody loves me. Aren't you happy for me? Aren't you my friend?

Believe or don't , i don't know what to really believe,but our never wrong psychic gave message from Luda from another side: If I knew then what I know now I would run for help.

She asked while in a form of skeleton. She asked to vindicate. She fell. And as if it's ok in an even voice said: i fell.

He wouldn't let me in their home. She was dying. I am just from airplane to see her, to help to care for her. He said NO.

She was dying and I was taking pictures of her windows. Numb. Still numb.

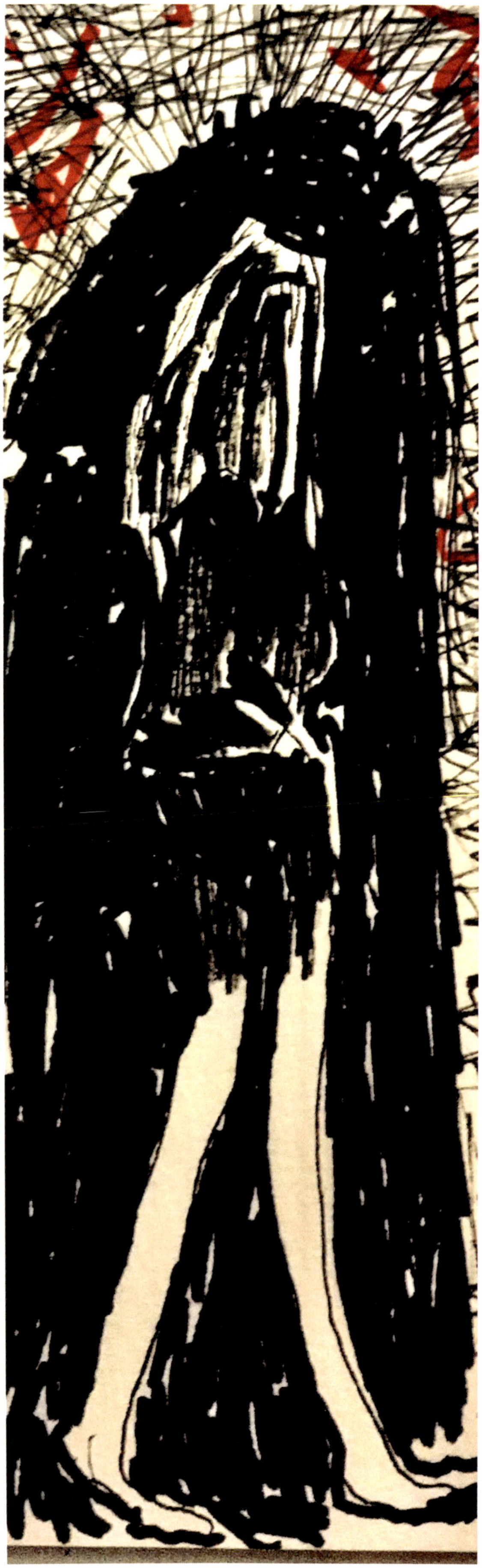

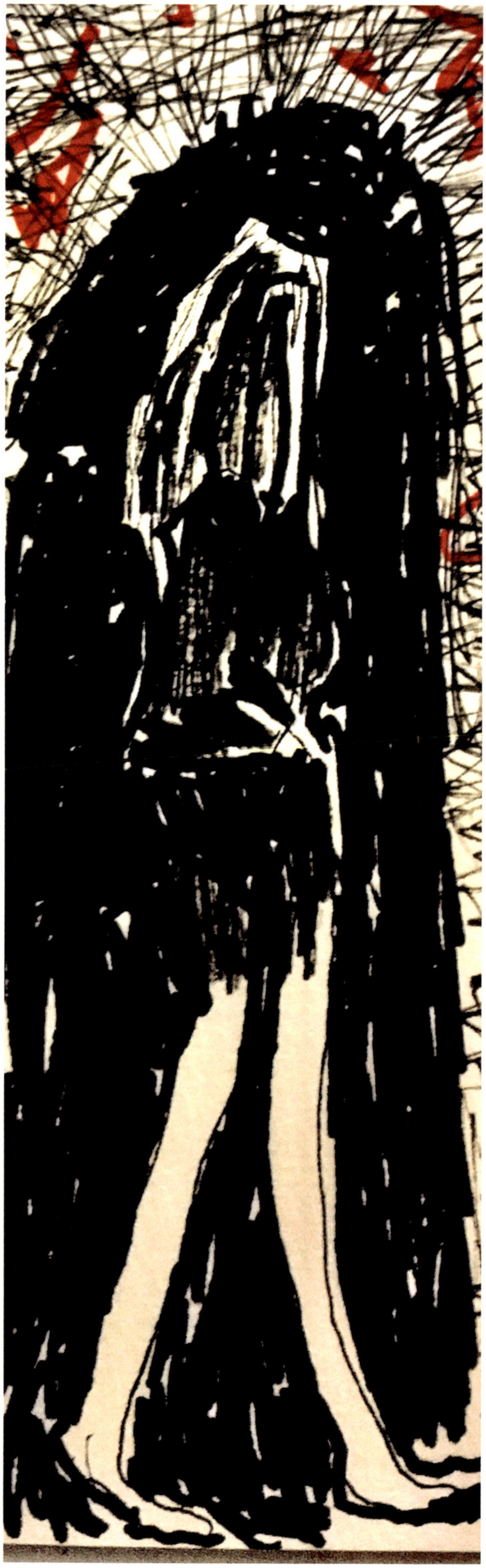

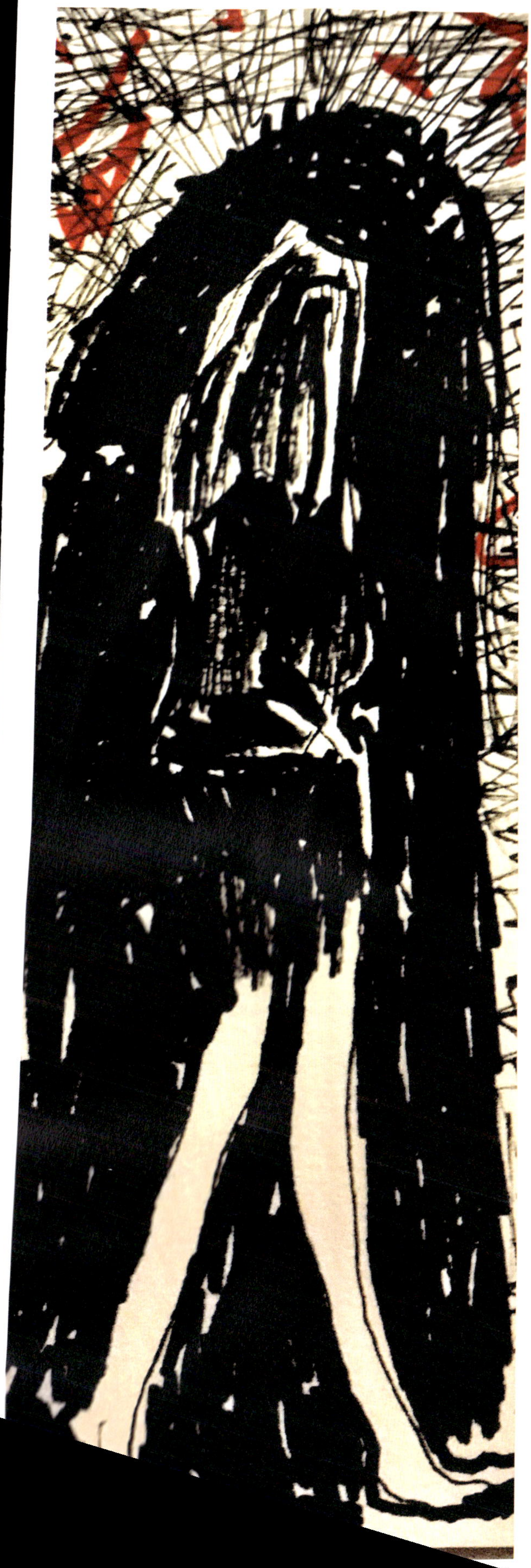
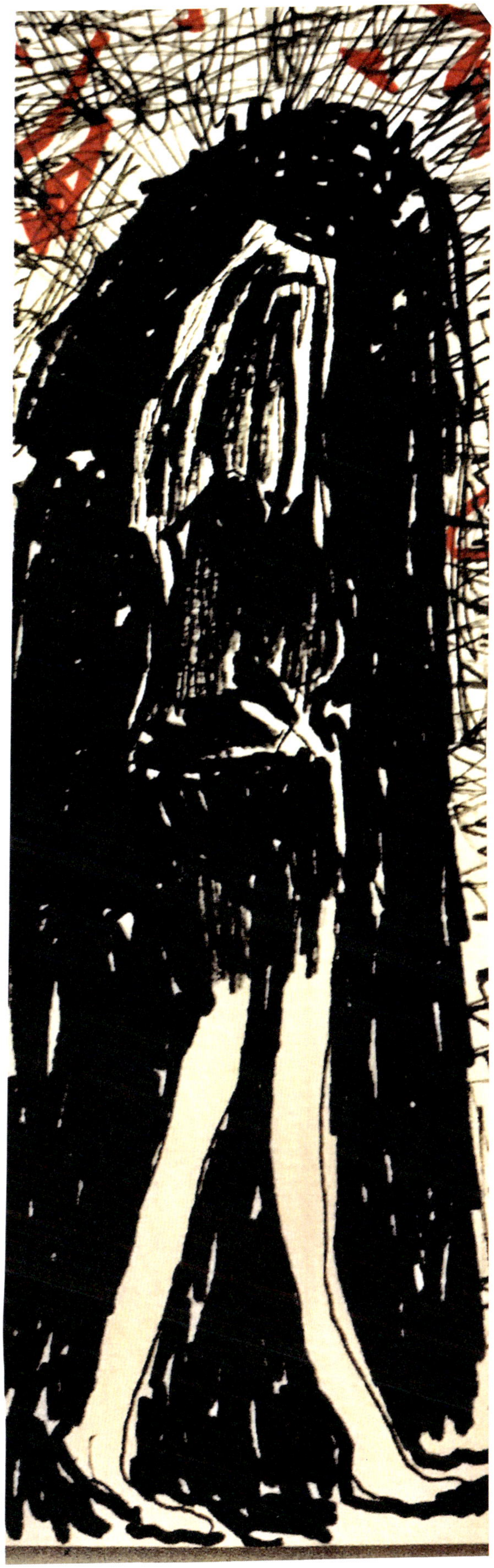

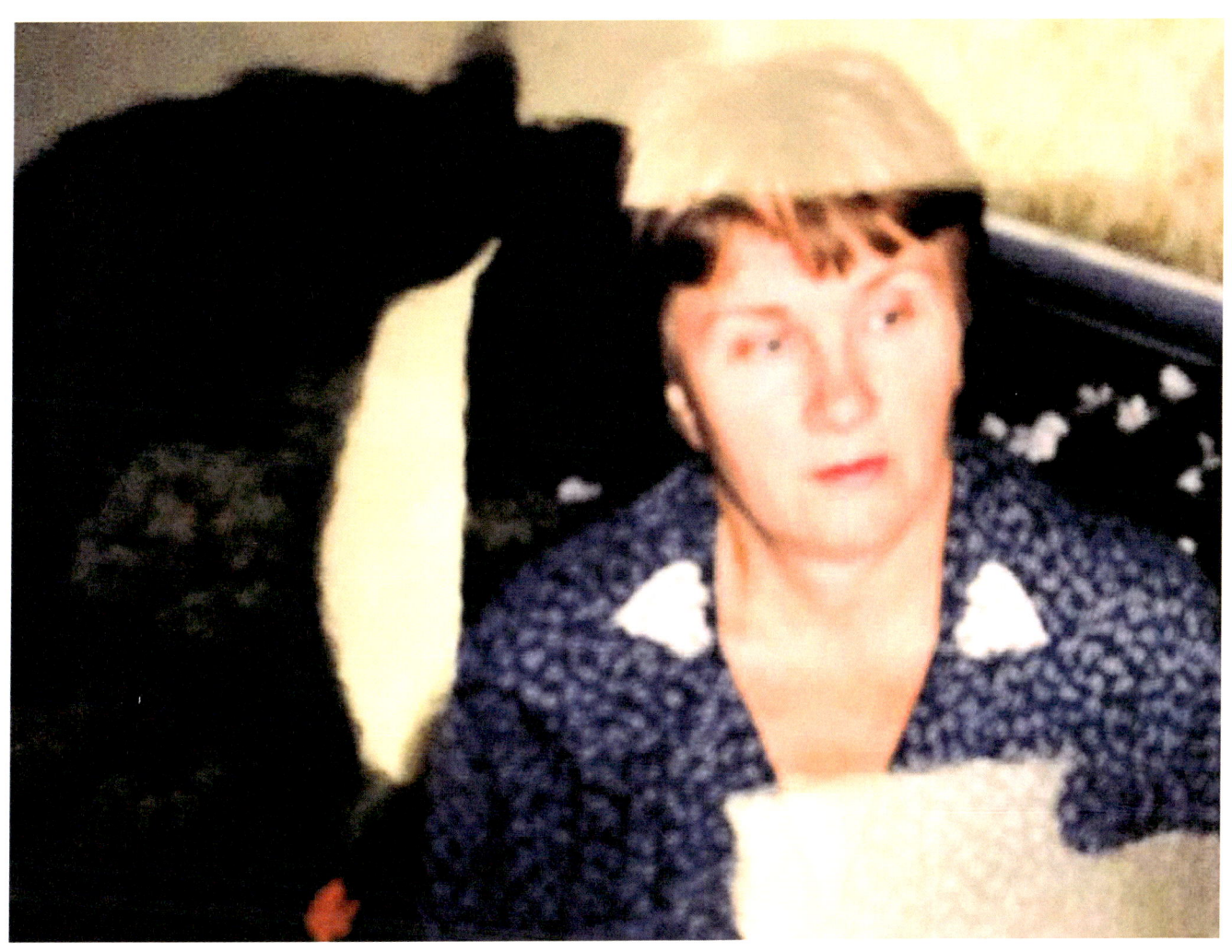

For there is nothing hidden that will not be disclosed, and nothing concealed that will not be known or brought out into the open.
Luke 8:17.

When i found out that your monster husband tortures you and and there is nothing can be done I propelled into the mental hospital. This is my art there.

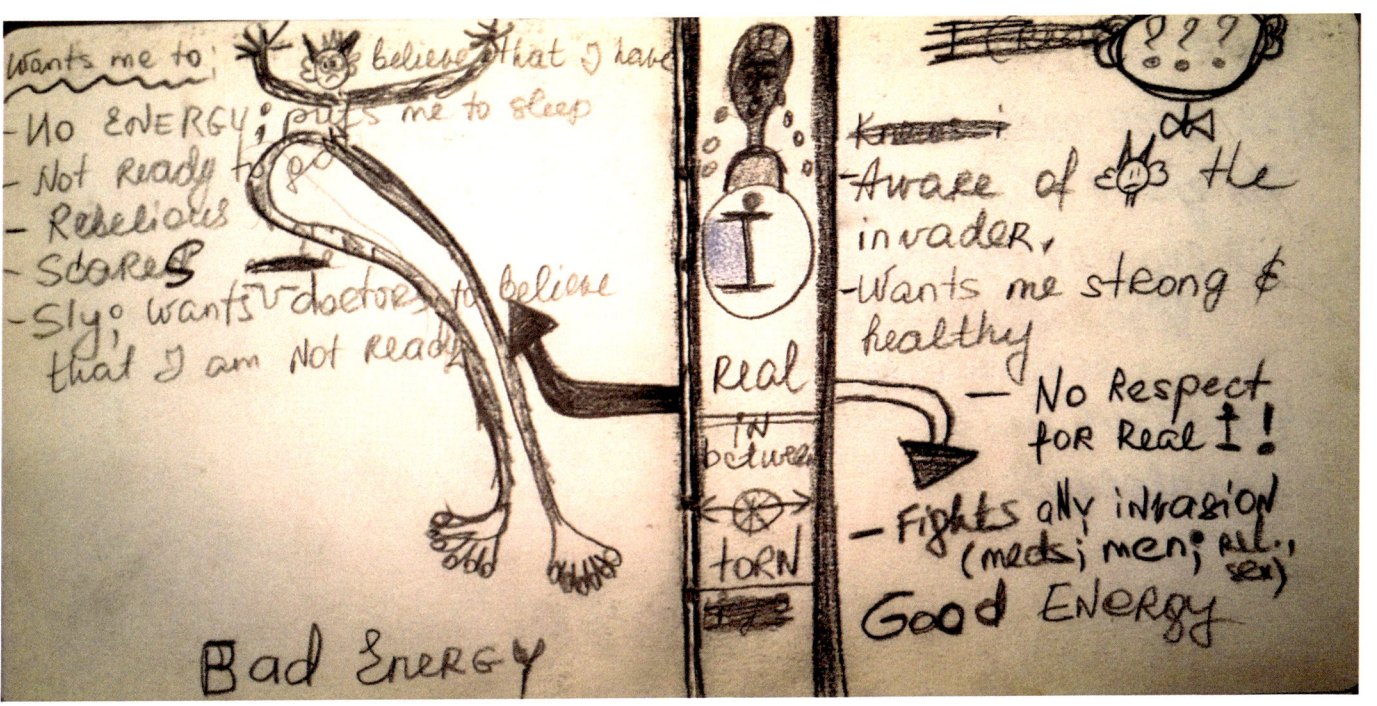

When you died in long tortures I suddenly found out how hard to tell this story. But I must. So this is the sorry I never knew existed and my Psyche runs around for 2 years. In a period of 2 weeks my sister, mom, and 3 animals dies. I adapted my father's tattoo: I don't believe in anything.

haha, Luda used to say: Sveta, out of all
humans and gods he hates you the most. And I
would say: Me? And we laughed. I am fluttered
i said.

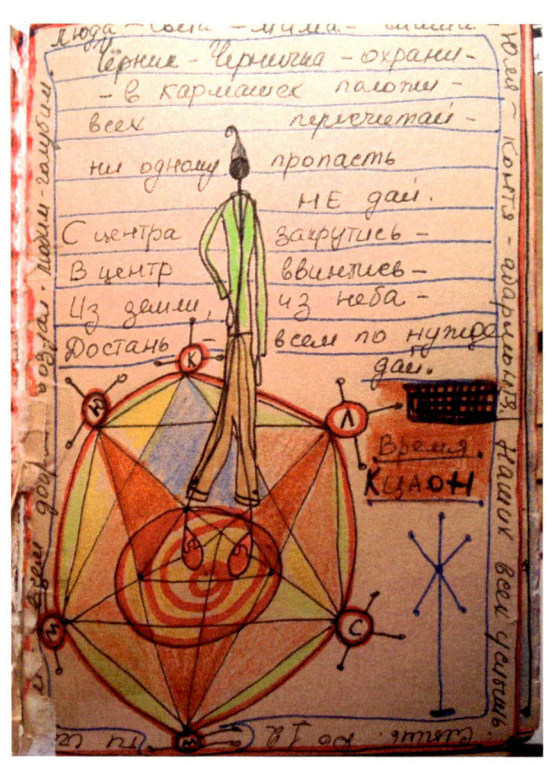

Jung said once or Freud that life of the family circles around the most troubled member. We all circled from one drama to another of theirs. Dad was sick, but no time for him. Luda in a drama. Mama running there all the time. Dad died, we lost him. Mom died 2 weeks after Luda. Luda's daughter took dad's side and literally kicked her with legs in hospice.

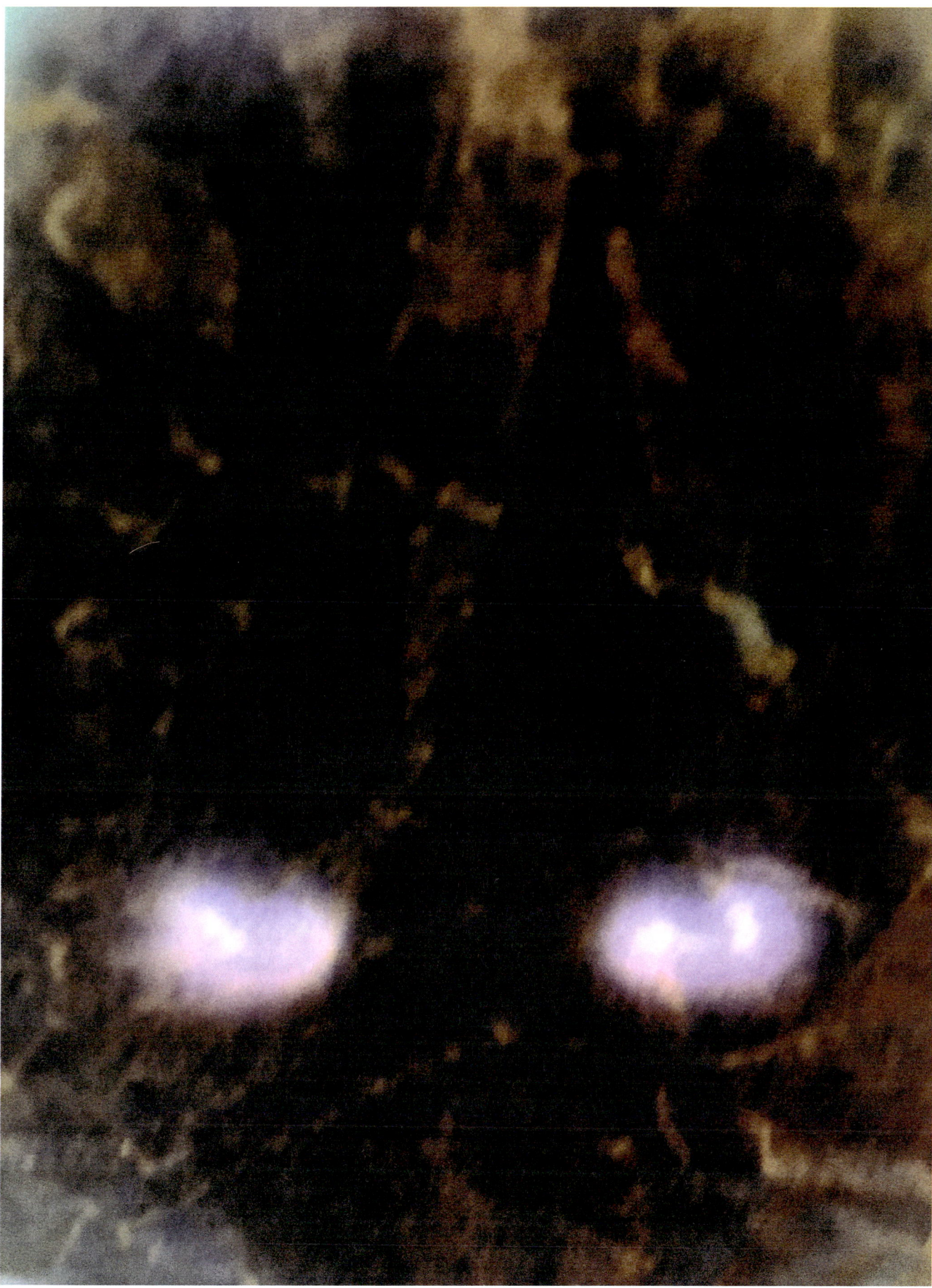

I came to you without me.
Come to me without you.
Rumi.

I will sing you petrifying song,
Maybe better even don't,
Don't listen.

She was so abnormally in love,
Made His Majesty God out of lover.

Bla-bla-bla - wedding.
Our father-captain,
Proud, noble man,
Knew this family well
And a little too late said:
Luda, if you don't become his wife,
I will stand on my knees, on my knees.
I am sure at the moment of that
He clearly was seeing.

How his child,
Will live in a Nazi camp,
With the psychological titan
With sophisticated methods.
All this so that she simply believed
He was doing angelic deed.

When i was little we grew up together. And I used to scream hysterically when i saw him. Nobody knew why, but i would scream for 30 min until i almost faint. He told us, when grew up that this scream he sees in nightmares all his life. So the name of the book " Scream for Borisov" his last name.

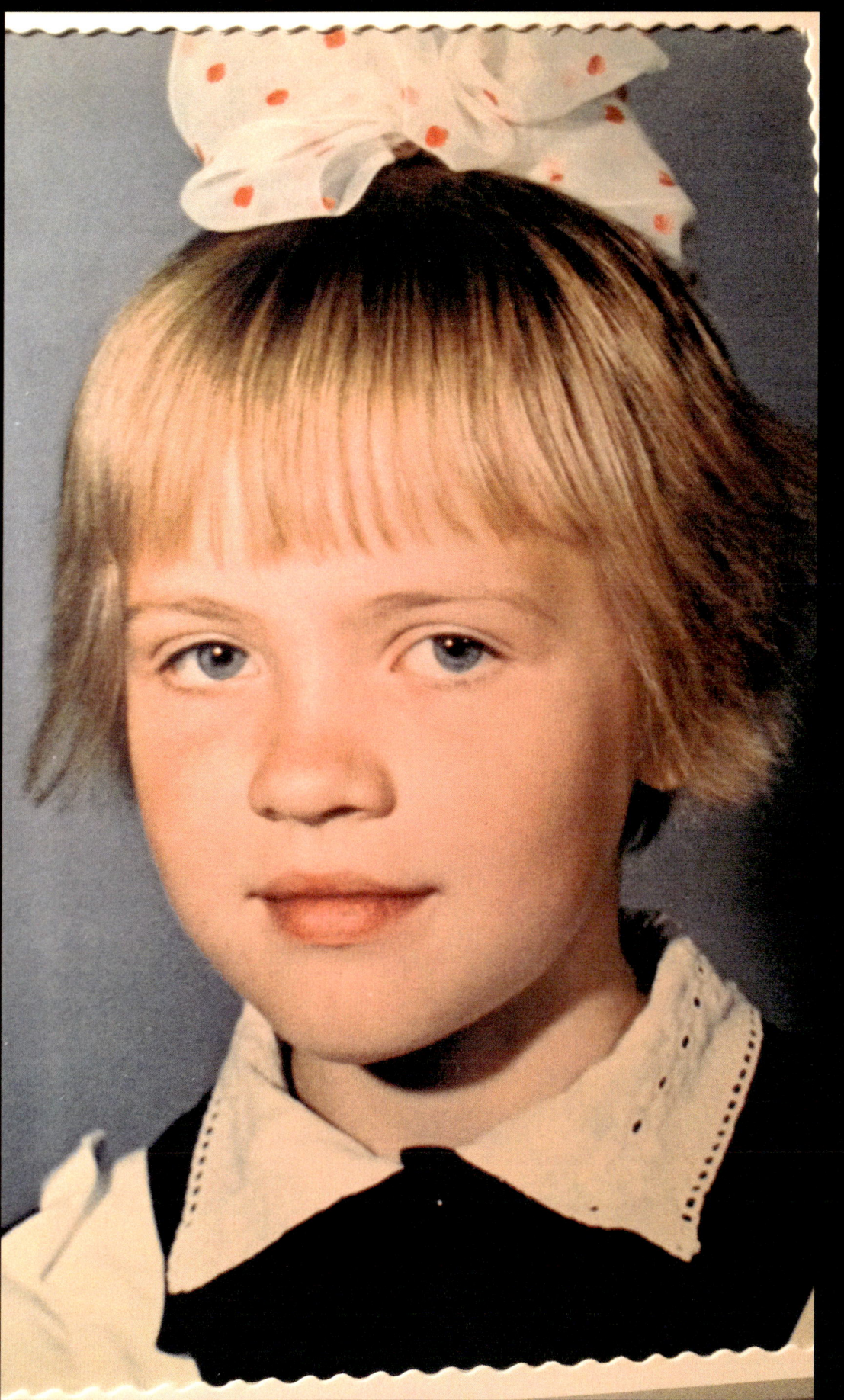

sveta, 2018.

Anyway the wind blows, doesn't really matter to me, to me.
Queen.
WHEN YOUR SISTER IS KILLED and only you know,
CAN ANYTHING REALLY MATTER.
In this book, that already out
Sveta whispers, smiles, gentle words -
How monster will soon be known,
Killing slowly, as an artist,
Surely sure secret dies, oh boy!
We were growing together,
Sveta screamed for no reason,
Every day and every time when his face in
Kindergarten.... no one could understand,
Why?
All his life in black nightmares, sweaty, heard he Sveta's scream.
Now, look at title of the book,
Luda, and a silent screaming Sveta,
Telling gently loudest and scariest to him that truth.

My life. Why do you keep bitting me up? Why do I live in a personal WW2?

Why 4 coffins in 2 month period? Each precious and loved.

Why my mom and sister were tortured by evil husband of Luda,

who's joy was to construct new and sophisticated psychological methods of torturing.

And fear of him was stronger then fear to die.

And why and how should I cary this on my shoulders?

When I try to convey this, people can't grasp such a horror.

It only happens in a horror movies.

When she stand in front of me, already just a skeleton I asked her:

Do you want me to vindicate you?

Her eyes showed fear, but she almost whispered "yes".

She was already in a hospice but he kept coming and whispering, controlling.

Every day. She used to be so fearless I felt embarrassed when i tried to compare

myself. Barefoot she was standing in front of him, right after the operation on

her brain. Bold and miserable. He was glowing with happiness. At this moment

he announced: I am loved! Somebody loves me. Arent' you happy for me?

I had to say it. To keep my promise to my little skeleton.

With the smoke
Up, up,
Thoughts ascending
To some gods, gods.
With two gulps of a gentle perfume
My piano is going nuts, nuts.

Thunderstorm screams in torture and rage.
Birds and animals hide, hide.
I don't know why, why
I am thinking of you my pain.

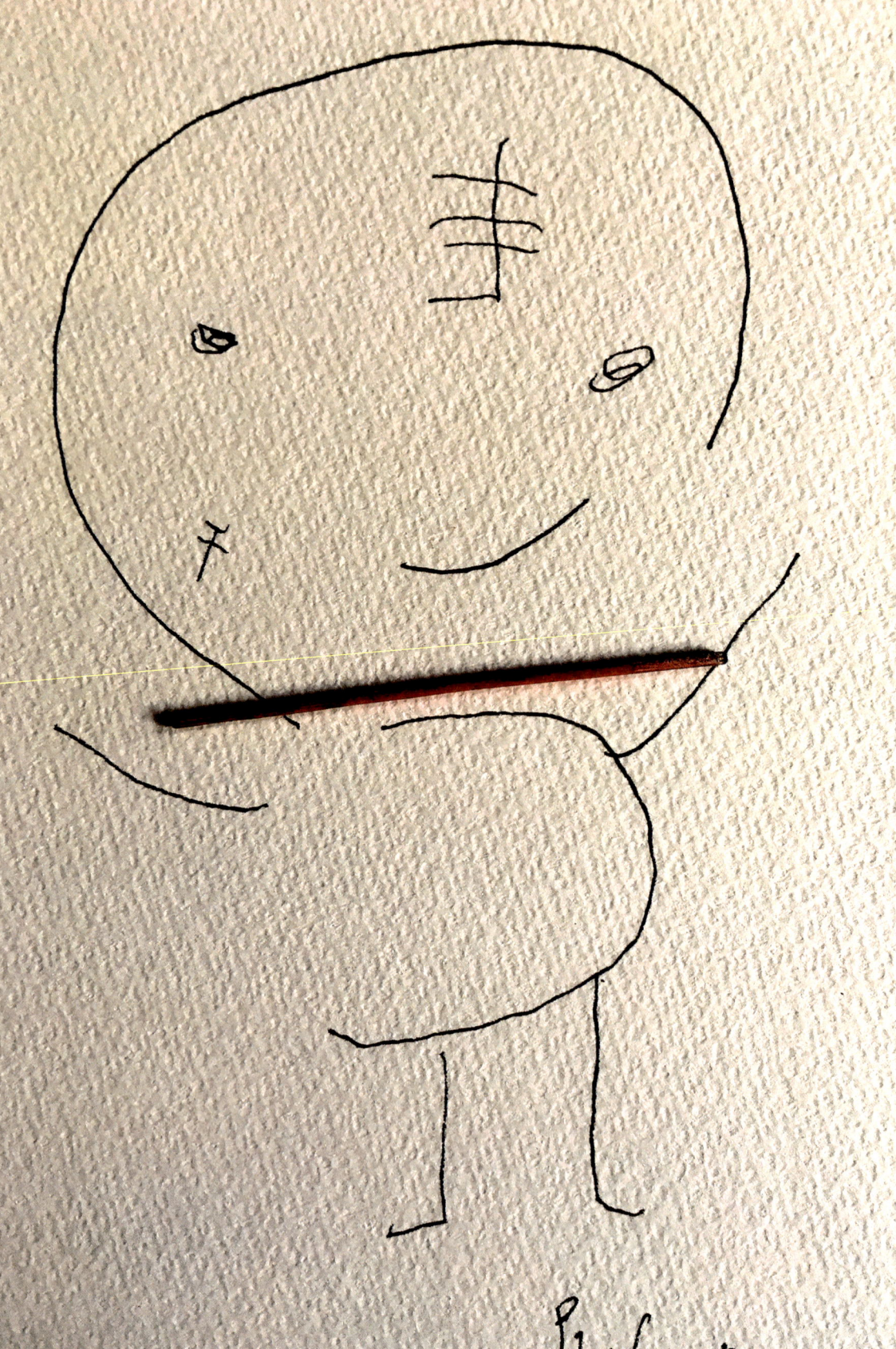

Neurosis is always a substitute for legitimate suffering.
C.Jung.

Then wow moved into the house. And the monster Borisov Yuriy lived in joy from Luda's pain. She was in hospice with spine's cancer and he was going to Maldive every second month with his new victim. He called every day: no body loves you, Sveta hates you but only in much more sophisticated way. She was very afraid. Of everything and everybody. But she said: when it's not something I can enjoy.

don't you find it super strange that i screamed at his presence at 5 y.o., he was 10? I must of forseen that.
and that he had nightmares about it all his life? Something similar happened to my dad. Proud like hell captain at their wedding he did something he couldn't explain: he said: Luda if you don't marry him i will stand on my knees.

the thing is nobody believed me. Nobody could grasp THIS montrosity. When I called to Hospital in Israel to find out how much longer she has, because he told us he iis not operatable and I was told: what? we never said that. And Julie said ankle Yura how could you do this? And he said: I don't have money. And she said: Every monet worth 250000$ in your collection. He screamed: not your business. Operation cost 30000.

That proved it. Till that happened i hoped it's not true. But after that me and Julie layed on the floor and buldozers were standing on us.

He could never NEVER say a nice word. Only snakes
came out of his mouth. His lover deserves it, she was in
Luda's store a manager. I knew right away what she
was. But I am scared for her

He said to Luda once: more than anything I am
afraid to become like my father. His father is
angel comparing to him. And I am grieving for that
boy who said that he is afraid to be like his father.

All the demons and gods are inside us.

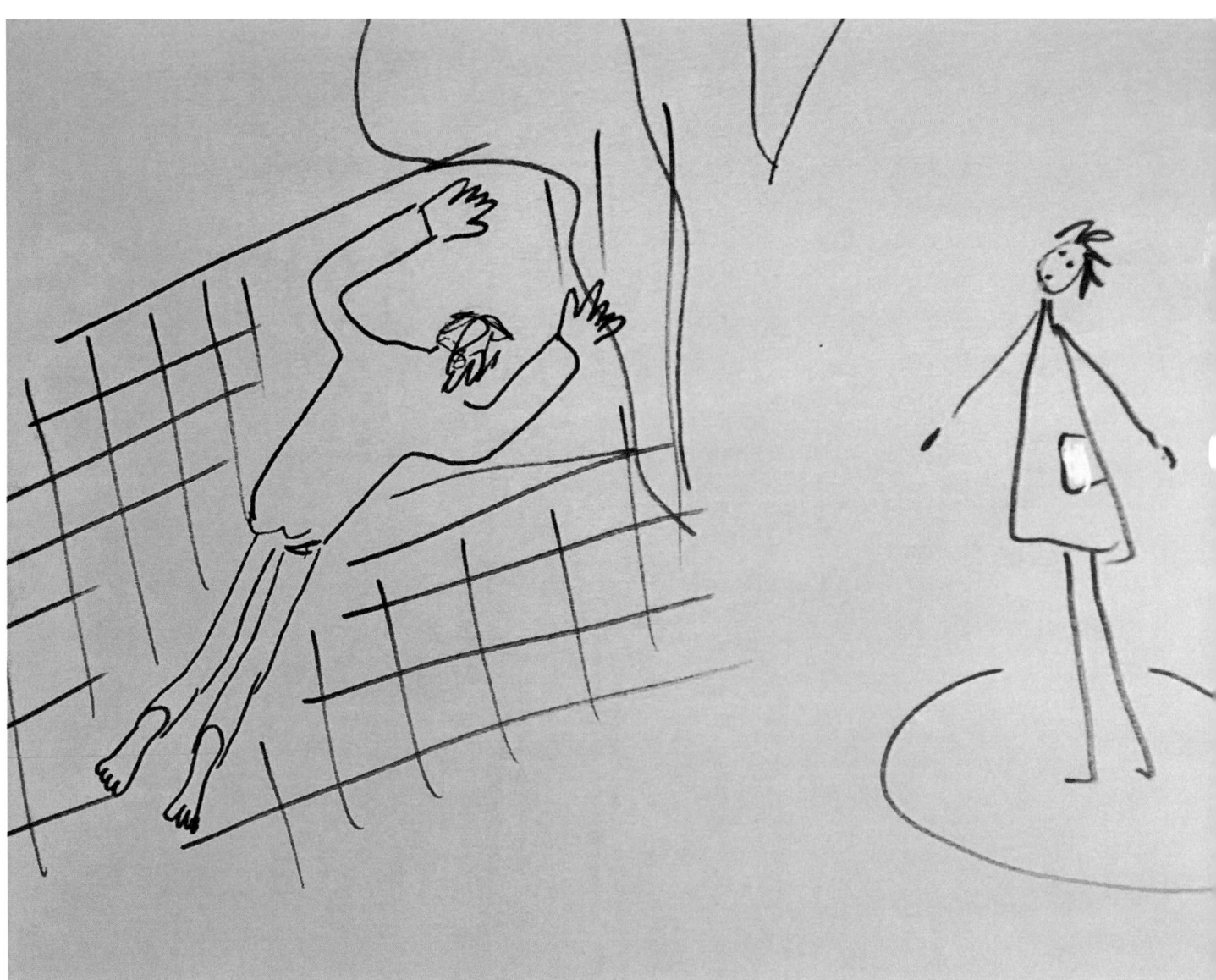

Do they have children?

oh, this is another tragic story. Jung said once or Freud that life of the family circles around the most troubled member. We all circled from one drama to another of theirs. Dad was sick, but no time for him. Luda in a drama. Mama running there all the time. Dad died, we lost him. Mom died 2 weeks after Luda. Luda's daughter took dad's side and literally kicked her with legs in hospice.

but this is truth: we all lived by each other. Like
one organism. Like crazy. Nothing mattered. We
were on Skype every day 25 years. all 5 of us.

The person who saved my life was
a very person I was running from.
(Dream)

Who cares what time, what year it is. It will be always 2 days ago from now on.

Sveta A; 2019
B.

As a doctor I am convinced that it is hygienic—if I may use the word—to discover in death a goal towards which one can strive, and that shrinking away from it is something unhealthy and abnormal which robs the second half of life of its purpose. ~Carl Jung, CW 8, Para 792

Anointing can be defined as "God on flesh doing those things that flesh cannot do". see II Corinthians 4:7 Someone who was anointed by God not only to [?] but also to be empowered by Him to the task or position to Which He Has called you.

OHEMEHUE ?

5 Ноября

ANOINTED

RB 2 Samuel

31 This God – Ris way [is] perfect; the work of Lord proves true; He is the Shield for All Those who Take R[efuge] in him!

RB = Sanders Web. net.

Hebrews 13:1-2

13:1 Let brotherly love conti[nue]
2 Do not neglect to show hospitality to Stran[gers] for thereby some ha[ve] entertained angels unawares.

Шаманы носили шапки наизнанку, высвобождая заблокированную энергию ~ нужную для совершения переход.

7 ASS – ОЗНАЧАЕТ "Бог" или "УСТА"… Сила этой Руны в[?] вобождает заблок. энергию, необход. для реал[изации] цели перемен. Дух внутри и вовне одно[вре]менно.

Psychology is a preparation for death. We have an urge to leave life at a higher level than the one at which we entered.

~Carl Jung; Conversations with C.G. Jung, Psychotherapy, Page 16.

The souls or spirits of the dead are identical with the psychic activity of the living; they merely continue it.

C.Jung. CW9i

Mighty is he who loves. But whoever distances himself from love, feels himself powerful.

~Carl Jung, The Red Book, Page 253.

"Life is tragic, and who doesn't know that didn't live"
C.Jung.

Art by Sveta A., inspired by Nelson.

S. Alexina Aug. 2015

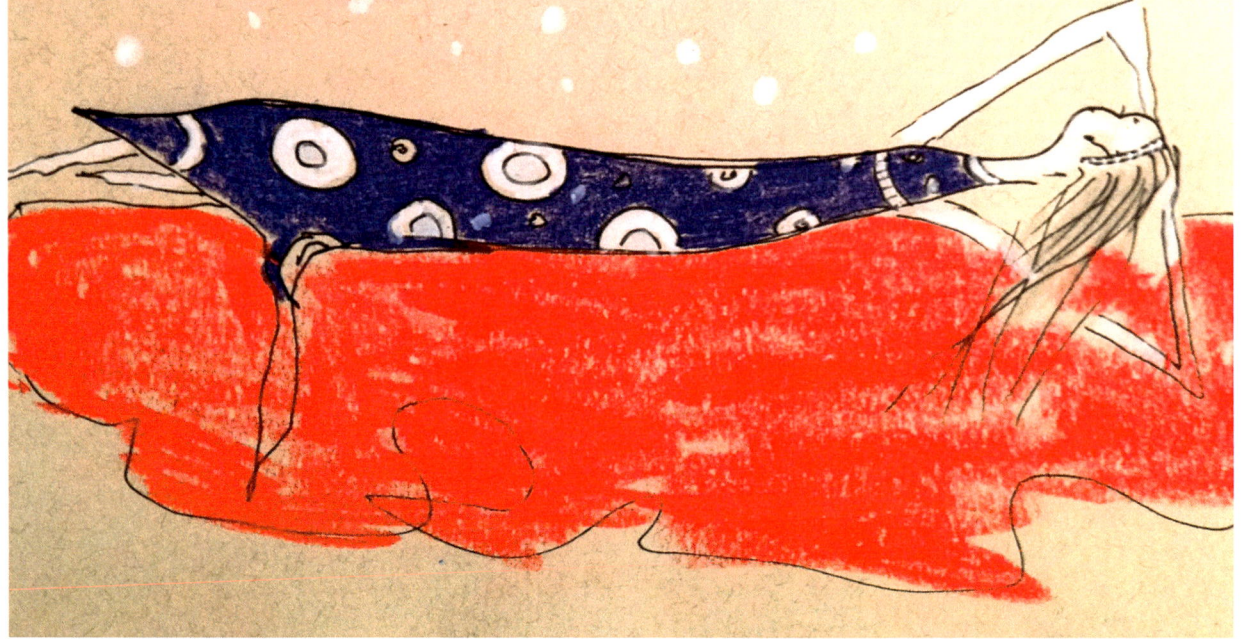

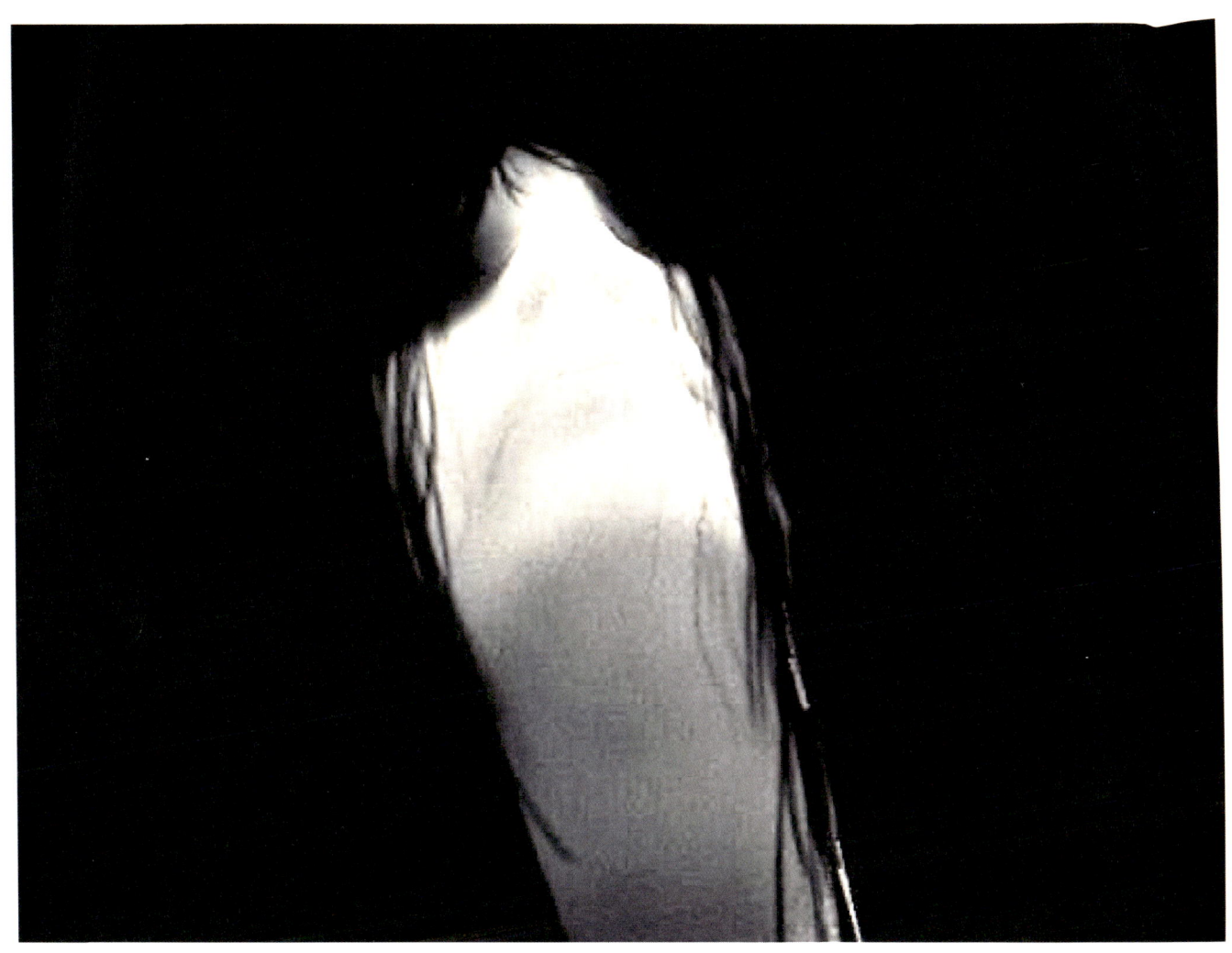

And I will become a which. And I
will heal the cows.

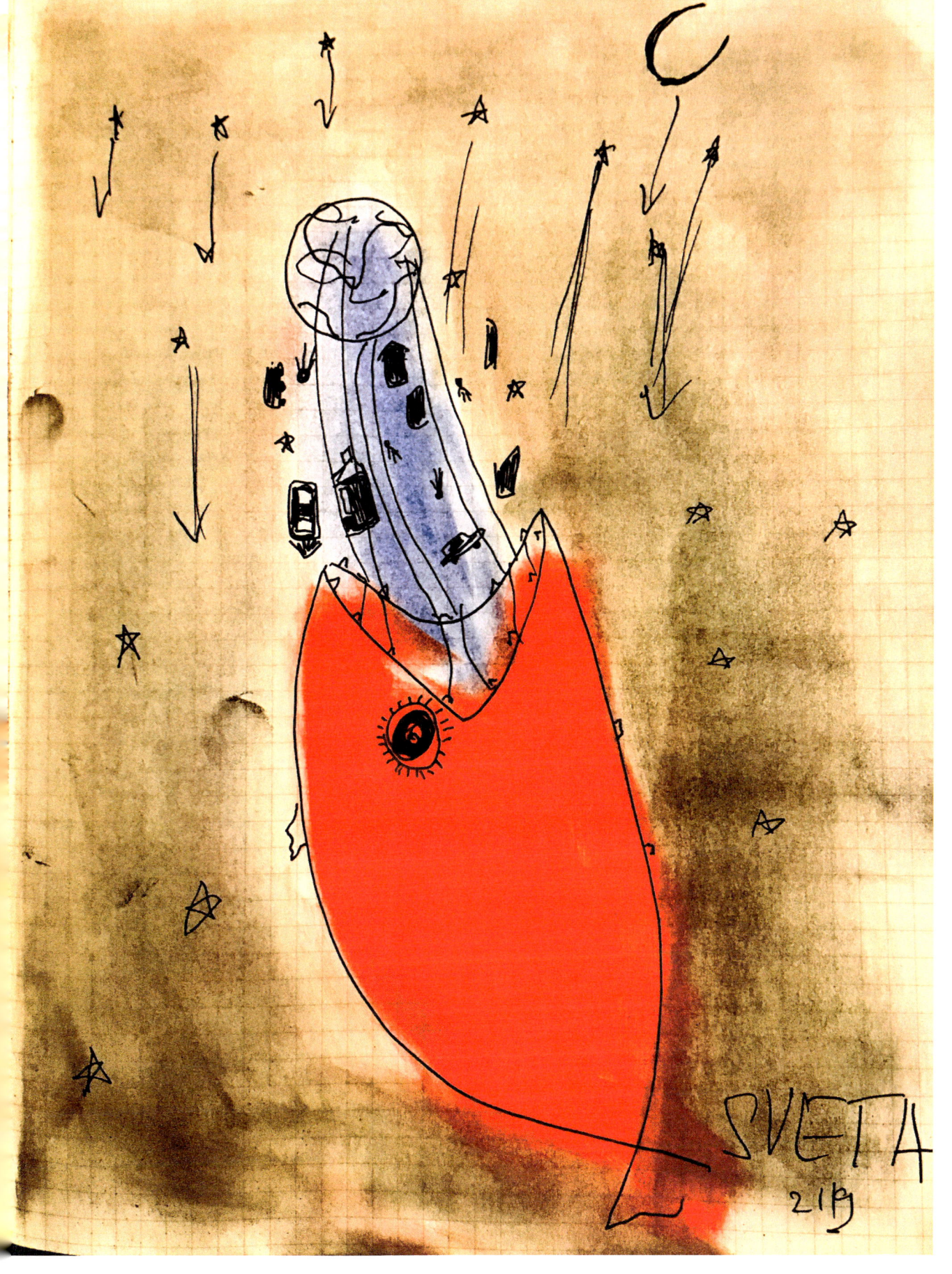

VERY TiRED CAT

sveta, 18

Pink wolf Bey.
sveta 2018

Hear me woolfy, hear me.
Gather all yours. All.

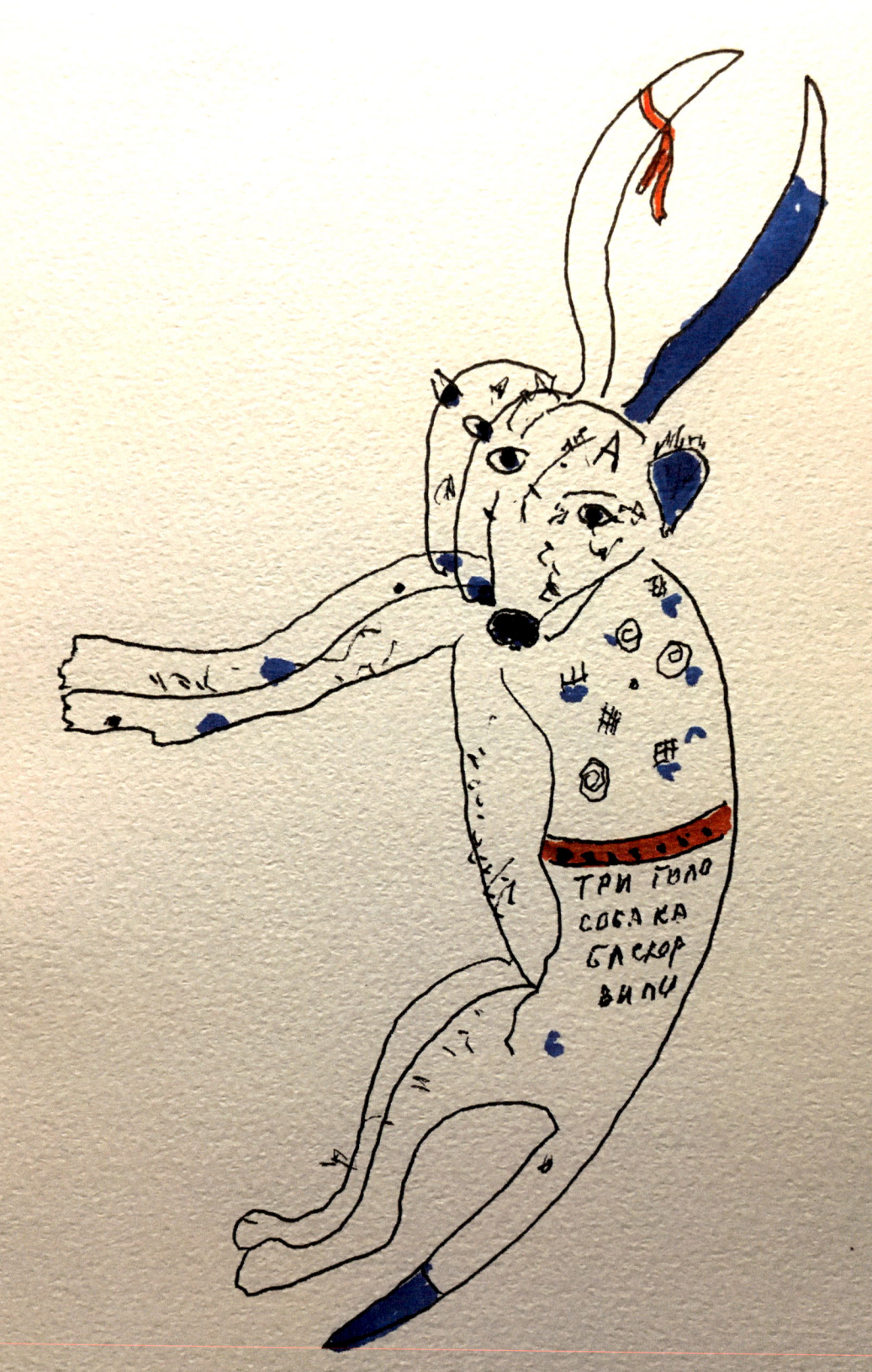

Anointing can be defined as "God on flesh doing those things that flesh cannot do". (see II Corinthians 4:7)
Somebody who was anointed by God not only to ached but also to be empowered by Him to the task or position to which He has called you.

[RB] 2 Samuel

31 This God - his way perfect; the word of Lord proves true; He is the shield for all those who take in him.

[RB] = Sanders Web. net.

Hebrews 13:1-2

13:1 Let brotherly love conti
2 Do not neglect to show hospitality to strang for thereby some ha entertained angels unawares.

ОНЕМЕНИЕ ?

5 Ноября

ANOINTED

Шапочки носили шапки нацнацу, восвобождая заблокированную энергию для совершения перемен.

Ass - ОЗНАЧАЕТ "БОГ" ИЛИ "УСТА"... Сила этой Руны вобогждает заблок. энергию, необход. для реал ции перемен. Дух внутри и вовне одно ременно.

Lightning Source UK Ltd
Milton Keynes UK
UKRC022019091019
351329UK00008B/204

* 9 7 8 0 3 6 8 8 5 8 7 0 3 *